YOU DON'T HAVE TO STRUGGLE

SPIRITUAL PRINCIPLES OF SURVIAL

WHILE PURSUING YOUR PURPOSE

Apostle Namon Wilson Jr. & Pastor Valerie Wilson

Motivational Speaker, Author Angel Ferguson

PRESENTS : YOU DON'T HAVE TO STRUGGLE

MARCH 18-20, 2016

Friday 7:30 pm

Saturday 10:00 am

Sunday 1:30 pm

LOCATED: NEW MACEDONIA MB CHURCH

3402 DELEUIL AVE. TAMPA, FL 33610

CONTACT ANGEL FERGUSON @ 813.516.4916

In this lifetime we are presented with an opportunity that some can only dream of, what an honor it is to have this awesome father/daughter team to present to you in a meeting of the minds some

spiritual & motivational insights of life!

We all face issues, being plagued with many struggles, as the desire to grow closer to God continues, in order to get back on the paths predestined for our lives, we must go through Christ, which is in all truths the only way!

It's amazing how we can place ourselves in inner struggles and ask the questions "Why and how did I get here"! The answer is simple,

we did not follow God's instructions.

There is a guarantee that as you sit and listen to the teachings of

Apostle Namon Wilson Jr., as He is being directed by God, that you will gain an understanding of the Kingdom-ship of Christ and how to take your rightful place in the presence of God.

And as there is no doubt that through the words of inspiration by

Motivational Speaker, Author Angel Ferguson, that it will cause you to take a closer look at the purpose of your life and how to make sure that your dreams, desires & journey are in-tuned with the plans

God has for you!

Epilogue

We are faced with some sort of struggle in one way or another. The examples below are just a few of the things that we have struggles with. Many can say you don't have to struggle but never tell you what directions to take to grow beyond the struggles of life!

I am struggling with things in my personal life because I do not want to accept my reality.

Looking at my surroundings, the thought comes to me that I could do better, but because I am used to having the minimum, I will continue to settle for less.

I am full of potential, very talented but I don't feel like getting out there, you know dealing with people.

I would love to give my children more, but they better accept what I have to offer. After all that's all my parents ever gave me.

My money is my money and I do with it as I please! But God, I bring my bills before you. I need help paying them.

Lord, I want to become a wife/husband but until then.

Lord, I want to be someone's first choice, but until then I will settle for this.

Dear God, I am struggling with my children, they won't seem to listen. They are in to all kinds of things.

Incept from Author Angel Ferguson

At 43, I am learning that my habits are just that my habits and not all of my habits are right. So within this book of motivation I wanted to examine the aspects of ones' life. How we say within that I love my family and the things my parents taught me but I know that there has to be a better way. A point has to come that you would like to know how to live on another street, where all the houses don't look the same.

As the days become available to me I am learning that all my struggles lead me back to God.

I am learning the meaning of I Corinthians 1:16, For in him all things were created: things in heaven and on earth, visible and invisible, whether thrones or powers or rulers or authorities: all things have been created for him and in him. As well as I Corinthians 8:6; yet for us there is but one God, Father, from all things came and for whom we live; and there is but one Lord, Jesus Christ, through whom all things came and through whom we live. Yes, I can give all my struggles to him.

We all have to find our own way in life. My path is not the path meant for the next man. What I am going after is how to bring my life totally in line with God's plans for me. Within his plans for me he reveals my simple self to myself. With even writing these words, there are some things that I am struggling with that are ever so present. Think it not by chance that we can write such a book and not look within. I can hear that whisper from God, I have you! I am holding you. I got you!

Incept from Apostle Namon Wilson Jr.

I have learned to seek the knowledge of who God is, what happened @ Calvary and whatever the word of God has to say. What has set me free is understanding Calvary and the Kingdom of God.

Question, do you understand Calvary and the Kingdom? Here in Matt 13:19 it states "Therefore speak I to them in parables: because they seeing see not; and hearing they hear not, neither do they understand."

People love God but have made a choice to put their trust in other things, and we will then get the wrong interpretations. The truth is that all scriptures are of God but not written by God. Man shall live by every word that comes from the mouth of God. Proverbs 16;1-5.

There are some secrets to obtain and here is one of them, what is Jesus teaching and who was He teaching? We must also have self-denial as no one will win the race unless they start it! Here is a another secret, faith and obedience must go hand in hand. We must have love which is the true foundation, faith and obedience in our lives.

Apostle Namon Wilson Jr.

To begin, let's look at the fact that in order to break any molds, we need to connect with our creator. What does God have to say about your life? What does God have to say about the reason he created you?

We are going to take a look at the following areas:

- Spiritual

- Family

- Self-Esteem

- Financial

- Careers

- Relationships

Within this book we will explore the areas of our lives and the things that we have and are struggling with. Once we overcome a certain thing, it will return. It's how you handle it that will determine your maturity. After all, dealing with struggles has to do with our maturity in Christ.

We pray that you apply the words within. Take a look at yourself and go before God for a full examination. I am learning to look at me allowing God to do the work in others. As the word does declare that we should seek our own soul salvation.

Apostle Namon Wilson Jr., & Motivational Speaker Author Angel Ferguson

It's not easy facing your realities, understanding that it was your way of doing things that has caused you to be in a struggle. You thought you had it all together but when the wind blew, it all came apart. Leaving you shaken, not knowing which way to turn because what you decided to build was done according to your way and not His. There is no scamming in Christ. There is a plan, a set of directions, a timetable & a time limit.

But, you went and followed the traditions of your parents or the habits of your friends because their way seemed quick & profitable on the outside. Let me share a truth with you, they will never describe the nights of struggling, worrying if that last idea will pan out. Hopping that no one will look beyond the surface to see that it was all put together with water and paste instead of an air tight glue!

We keep trying to veer off of the path of our predestined paths only to leave debris behind. But does this stop some of us from trying to move ahead? No. One thing is for sure, before we can move on we must clean up our trails. Without cleaning up what we let fall to the wayside, our next level will lack stability.

How can I stop this merry go round? Or better yet, when will I become tired of hitting this brick wall? If only I would learn to follow those instructions to the letter instead of asking for the opinions of others. Yes, they went before me but that was their path and they had their own set of directions!

We can not afford to model our expectations based of the next man's progress or failures. For if I give you my way of doing things, it is indeed my way! Ask yourself, where will my way lead you? After learning of my way are you willing to push as I did? Are you willing to endure the set backs that I have experienced? Why not follow the path of God so that you don't have to go through the bumps and bruises that I did. We can share our experiences but this day, I implore you to follow the one that has created you? You see, we might have a hidden agenda that will not want you to surpass us! Yes, you just read that correctly, it's in our nature not to want others to go beyond us. It takes a genuine love of Christ to really want the best for others. Not sure why we do this, we have a tendency to provide half of the details, and I truly believe that's why the word of God declares that one plants, one waters but it is God that gives the increase. He knows our nature therefore He has given one person so much authority or knowledge to share, if you will.

SPIRITUAL

REFERENCE SCRIPTURES ON SPIRITUAL GROWTH & MATURITY

Colossians 1:9-10

1 Peter 2:1-25

2 Peter 3:18

Matthew 5:6

Galatians 5:22-23

Ephesians 4:15-16

Psalms 1:1-3

Philippians 1:6

Philippians 4:13

2 Timothy 3:16-17

2 Peter 1:5-8

1 Corinthians 11:1

James 1:1-27

Titus 2:11-14

Ephesians 4:12-13

Hebrews 6:1-3

Hebrews 10:24

Hebrews 5:12-13

John 4:14

At one point or another we have all struggled when it came to our spiritual lives, whether it was in the beginning of your walk with Christ or when we just did not have a clear understanding of what the scriptures were saying unto us. It is so important to develop a relationship with Christ so that as we read and mediate on His word, we will gain a truthful understanding and not the understanding of what our natural man wants to understand. This is such a delicate area, when we think about a spiritual struggle.

Not all things that come up against us are struggles.

Some are just a test to see if we have grown in faith. To see if we are really living the words that we share with others. I have gained the understanding that when things in my life keep going in a unprogressive circle, that it is something that I am not paying attention too. It's true, there are times that things will circle back around because for one, we have not learned the lesson. It could be because we have lost faith and are starting to waiver at the promises of God. This walk is daily, it's not something that we can pick up and use only when it is convenient.

Sometimes we struggle because we don't have an understanding of where we are or where God is leading us too. Then there are those times that we struggle because we just won't head to the warnings that were sent previously. There are so many reasons why we have struggles spiritually, this list is endless and to be honest, who can actually pinpoint them all? The truth is, the only way to understand why we have a spiritual struggle is to seek God.

Here is something worth sharing, I had the weirdest dream last night. I was on a business trip & for some reason I was taking care of someone's infant.

Within this dream I found myself carrying some extra baggage. This extra baggage was needed to care for this infant along with my own personal things. I found myself with a baby in one arm while trying to pull my laptop bag, hold a purse and trying to walk, all at the same time.

There was even a suitcase that was meant to stay behind, but I was trying to figure out how I could grab that too! There was one thing that I did noticed and it was that the parents of this infant were hands free, while I was handling the load alone! Yes, they were in a clamed and controlled state, with not a care in the world.

This dream was so real, it was on my mind while I dressed for work, drank my coffee and during my commute.

The truth is, I've been sitting here at my desk all morning thinking about this dream, waiting on an answer. Waiting on God to give me some insight. Not my insight but the truth. I know it has to be spiritual & nothing of the natural!

So I just waited, then as I was sharing it with someone, the revelations came. Here it is, I, we can take on things that do not belong to us out of nothing more than doing a good deed.

The truth is, we can't carry someone else's load!

We can offer encouraging words, keep others in prayer, share experiences etc., but your load is your load as my load belongs to me....So throughout my day, I am asking God to reveal to me what I have picked up that does not belong to me, so that I may give it back in love! Encouraging you to do the same, let's stop taking on the things that do not belong to us!

On the next few pages, please to take your time and consider the things that you are struggling with spiritually. This is something you can do in the privacy of your own home or in a group discussion. We encourage you to be real as there is no surface answers or shall I say easy answers. We encourage you to take these things to God as He is the only one that can help us to become overcomers.

_____

_____

_____

_____

_____

_____

_____

_____

_____

_____

_____

_____

_____

_____

_____

_____

_____

_____

_____

_____

_____

_____

_____

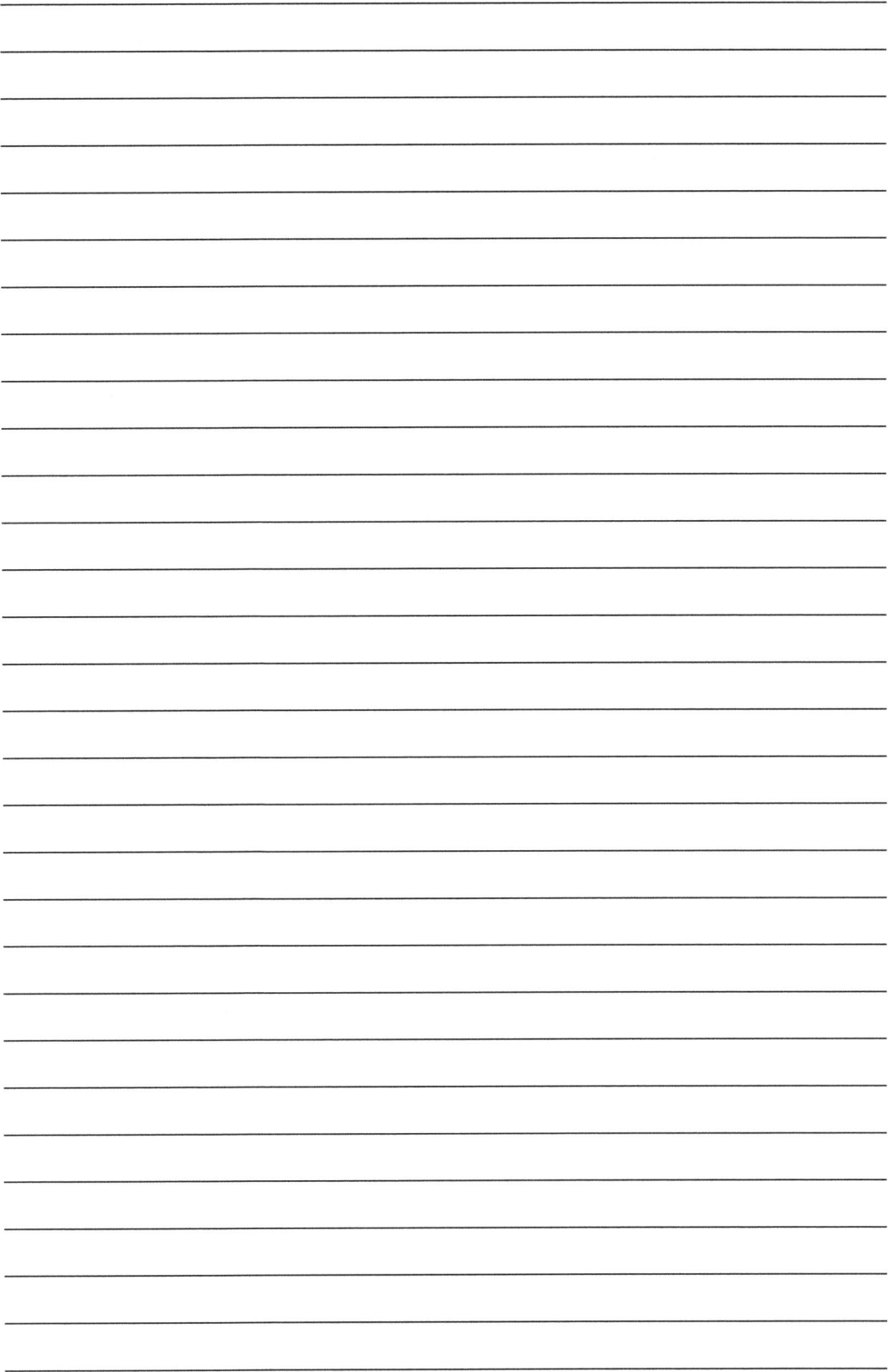

FAMILY

REFERENCE SCRIPTURES ON FAMILY

1 Corinthians 13:1-13

1 Corinthians 13:4-7

2 Corinthians 6:18

1 Timothy 5:8

1 John 4:19

Exodus 20:12

Proverbs 22:6

Philippians 4:13

Psalms 127:3-5

Ephesians 5:28

Ephesians 5:33

Breaking the mold of the family's tradition of drama. Even as Abram was instructed to come out from among them., in order to pursue his lands of milk and honey we must do the same.

At what point do you look over your life and make a contentious decision that you want more for your life? At what point do you come to realize that the things that were passed down to you, meaning the lessons of life are not leading you in the right direction? Is there a point that you look outside of your box and realize that there is another way of living? At what point do you look long and hard at the group of people you call friends and realize, that everyone in the group is in the same boat of going nowhere?

No one has a conversation about goals, no one is having a conversation about achieving anything, but only about the struggles of their parents and are hence forth passing on this same conversation to their children. There has to come a point that there is an yearning within that you want more! There has to be something inside of you that cries out, "I saw my parents struggle, beg and borrow and now I am doing the same things.

It can start with something as simple as your parents telling you to go borrow some eggs from the neighbor. Please understand that this example reaches beyond the example of borrowing eggs.

It goes to our children going outside of the home for advice or a mentor. Is there a point within you that would like to have pride in being the provider for your family?

As parents, we should have a desire to provide more than a roof, meals & clothes. What about values, morals, the importance of a good education, the list is endless.

The truth is I had to learn a valuable lesson the hard way, I assumed my children were watching me as an example. Yes, I sat down and talked with them but now I can see there are some things I was doing in error that have been adopted within their actions today.

It's funny that we see a lot of our errors when one of our children become adults, we try to catch the younger siblings before they go down the same road.

Here is something else that is not so funny, we can see the wrong turns of someone else's child or in another person but will not have a clue that we are in the same position.

How is that I can see that your family has no bread when mine has no beds? The point is not trying to make one better than the other. It's not what we possess but about the one whom is our provider.

What I find now is that I am trying to capture every moment of wisdom that comes my way, as long as it measures up with the word of God. There is no definite answer as to why it takes us so long to finally grasp what it means to be a parent, it's true that we learn along the way but if we would take pride out of the way, it might not take so long to apply the lessons.

Here is something to consider, ask yourself "what am I really giving my family" ? During some recent conversations with my mother Pastor Valerie Wilson, she is on a mission for her children, grand children and great-grand children to know her! She has a desire that we all know the things that make her the person she was and has become. She wants to give us Christ, yes introduce us to the truth that she has found. As I listen to her, I am understanding that she wants her family to know the real her, the things that make her smile and the things that make her cry. Another thing is being done here, she is making sure that for generations to come, the name "Nanny" is known not just by name but by face and actions of love.

SELF-ESTEEM

REFERENCE SCRIPTURES ON SELF-ESTEEM

Genesis 1:27

Roman 7:5

Romans 8:35-39

Ephesians 3:17-21

John 3:16

Mark 12:31

Mark 12:30

Proverbs 12:18

1 Peter 3:3-4

1 John 3:1

Jeremiah 29:11

Matthew 16:24-25

Matthew 11:28-30

We wanted to cover an area that is so often missed or taken for granted. That area is low self-esteem

If we are really going to face the truth, then we must all accept that we struggle with issues with our self-esteem. I do not believe there is a person alive or that shall live that will question their abilities because someone did not give a second hand to our decisions. We tend to look for the approval of others when we do not know or even understand our value and worth. We will accept the opinions of others without appreciating what we have to offer.

Then there is that divine question, what or who does God say that I am? What does he see in me? And then again, can I see myself as He sees me?

How can He look beyond all my faults and yet, daily I allow myself or someone to remind me of the things I did wrong in the past. After all he created us all. So therefore if he created me and knows all about me, then why can't I trust and accept the good that he sees in me. Why does another opinion matter, when he created them too?

Wait! You mean to tell me that he created us all yet, for some reason we as a people want to point out the flaws of the creations that we had no control over. But wait. What are you saying? I am saying that if you do not like who I am or what I have become, take it up with the one that created us both. Let's see how far you get when you go to God and cast your thoughts on what he made. What he desired to be upon this earth. Come back and tell me his reply. Come back with the stones that you could not cast because to cast them at ones self is not wise!

I have come to realize that low self-esteem is a trap. It is a trap to keep you from wanting to know your purpose upon this earth. It's a trap from keeping you from wanting to dream of a better life for yourself and your family.

Here is a prime example of the trap of low self-esteem; You look at the needs of yourself and your family. You would like to get a better job. Within you want to work in an office atmosphere. You have a desire to change the type work you have done previously but you decide not to go for it for the following reasons: don't have the right clothing, I won't fit in with them, etc. Let me tell you, it's a trap!

I say it's a trap because you are hindering your growth by not making an effort. You don't have the right clothing, change what you buy! Think you won't fit in? Learn to fit in. Figuring that you can't follow the conversation or unable to add to it. Instead of catching up on the celebrity gossip, catch up on some world events.

With low self-esteem, comes with the willingness to easily trust. It's not that they take so much from you, it's your low self-esteem that started giving things up in the beginning.

Therefore you have set the expectations of giving one ownership of what you have. Learn to look over the patterns of your previous relationships from the beginning to the end. Learn to recognize the structure of your process of meeting people. Stop being so giving of yourself so quickly. You're giving people the tools to walk off and leave after you give, leaving you with nothing! Just as they came, with nothing but making you feel as if you should be grateful for their attention. You're giving up your self- respect is their reward for paying attention to you.

Ask yourself, do you have standards? Yes, you put it all out there, without them having to ask for anything. Presenting yourself as the perfect package when in fact you're broken within. You're insecure. For once allow someone to learn of your qualities, to earn your value.

When it comes to dealing with self-esteem, people are carriers. Yes, people will sit and observe you, will learn of the things that you do not like about yourself and then point them out to you.

People will go as far as to tell you that someone you've never met pointed out the same thing and will have the nerve to come and tell you about it! This is what it means to become a carrier.

They carried the information out and carried back the negativity. Here is one thing that I have learned, a praise report will travel slow but a report of harsh words and judgements will fly like a speeding bullet.

Throughout the years, I have had numerous conversations with my mother Pastor Valerie Wilson about self-esteem and how it has affected her. The truth is that it starts long before we enter into this world. It's how our parents perceive us to be when we are born. Once we are born, our beauties as well as our flaws are pointed out. Yes, they are announced to the world and each time we are introduced to a stranger or family member those attributes are noted. What we all have failed to realize is that through this action we have given the first complex of how a child sees themselves. How does your son know that he did not walk as quickly as the others and must be a little behind in the process unless he has heard it repeatedly?

Now he has developed in his mind that he can't keep up with the others, which will trickle into his progress in school, his adult life, relationships, etc. Until one day when he is seeking God about this life and the things that God would have him to do, and it is revealed that God has a plan for each of us to go at His pace and not ours!

Until we realize that we were not meant to be perfect in the eyes of man but in the eyes of God, we are nothing but love, created in His image. The bigger question is this, who but God has a clear understanding what is meant by being created in the image of God but God himself? It is not our outer appearance that is in the image of God but our spirit man, that's what's important.

Let's look at the process of building self-esteem.

Building ones' self– esteem is also about changing ones atmosphere. Learn to change your surroundings. Learn to study where you desire to be then begin to implement those positive changes in your life. Learn to put aside the immature things of your life.

Change the atmosphere of your household one step at a time. I am not saying to become someone else or to model your life like your neighbor but take the things you admire and make your own adjustments.

INDEPENDENCE

Independence tells me that yes, I am judged often by the color of my skin yet I have limited myself with my way of thinking. Here is something that I have observed, no matter how much money you may have, your social status, where you live, what you wear etc., if you have a mentally of being stagnate, then that is where you shall remain.

If you have a spirit of always borrowing from others, make an effort to stop. Yes, borrowing is a self-esteem issue! It says that you are not willing to make changes in your life to do better, therefore you will sit back and ask of others. Well, I must say what's wrong with you! I am giving you were I came from...........and have no desire to return.

Let me share this. I used to have this bad habit of every time my sister would pick me up, I needed to stop and do this or that. Not realizing that it was an inconvenience. Or I needed to get ready at her house for a house party. Then one day, I pulled my own shirt tale and said no more. No one else is responsible for me and how I make things come together.

Once you discover your purpose in this life and you begin your journey you will discover that it is about accepting the reality of you.

The thing about your journey is that it's not about an observation of the faults, weaknesses & shortcomings of others but about you!

A journey is simply a road map of your life, where you have been, where you are & where you are heading.

A journey is not an opportunity for us to become so elite in status that we hunger for the ways to become judgmental of others but to me it's a way of seeing me.

How at one point I had it all under control only to realize that all things had control over me. Or that my complaining was simply a testimony that I was not willing to make some positive changes.

Yes, this journey is more than about career moves, new business ventures or expanding one.

This journey is about maturity! Maturity tells me that this world owes me nothing. Yet reminds me that I owe the world the opportunity to appreciate my gifts and talents.

If your journey has you looking down on others, I encourage you to evaluate your map! If your journey has you thinking you are better than,

yes evaluate that too!

The truth is in order to survive the journey, we must become as students that are willing to forever learn as well as forever willing to teach others along the way.

CAREERS

REFERENCE SCRIPTURES ON CAREERS

Jeremiah 29:11-14

Proverbs 3:5-6

Proverbs 16:3

Proverbs 18:16

Proverbs 19:21

Proverbs 24:27

Psalm 1:1-2

Psalm 32:8

Psalm 37:4

Joshua 1:8

Jeremiah 17:7

James 1:1-27

John 3:27

1 Timothy 4:8

Romans 8:28

Ecclesiastes 9:10

My Monday morning question, "Now that this day is upon you, are you prepared for it?"

I often say, let's take this day by storm but if you are not prepared there could be a delay or you might not experience the full effect you were expecting.

Nothing just happens, we must all prepare to become a better us!

It will never just happen overnight without recognizing our shortcomings, putting them aside and taking on some new methods.

What I am learning daily is that just because it is my habit does not mean it is the right method or the best method.

I must admit that when I do things on a whelm, something is missed, overdone and even at times unnecessary.

In all that we set out to do, let's keep this in mind "A prefect presentation of you, takes preparation!"

You are your best investment, biggest supporter & highest critic! After examining yourself, would you buy what you have presented?

I recently had a conversation with someone that was contemplating on giving up on their dreams of having a business. It was not because of the clients or the heavy work load, it was because of the lack of support by loved ones. In this journey you, we must come to the reality that the vision, dream & desire is not to those around you but you! If your drive is based off of someone pushing you then you are only entertaining a hobby and fulfilling a need to be seen.

Pursuing your dreams is something that goes beyond the surface & will not allow you to let go just because someone did not pat you on the back. This journey calls for long walks alone! It calls for silence in prayer! It requires patience and confidence in yourself! It calls for you relying on the plans that God gave you not the suggestions of those that have dared to go where you have been! Today, push & hold on to that passion within you! As all things take time to grow, don't give up before your harvest has had a chance to show of your works.

This journey calls for some amazing changes in maturity. Before I can comprehend the next move, I must gain control of my current atmosphere.

Gaining the reality of where you are in your present state of mind will help to determine where you desire to be in the future.

How can we move to another room without closing all the doors and securing the windows?

For if I leave a window of opportunity open, the wind will be sure to follow me and I don't know about you but I am not a fan of unexpected, strong gusty winds!

Simply because I believe that we all have great potential within us. It's when you can learn to recognize it, appreciate it, and use it for the good that counts!

So today, I want to encourage you not to give up on the potential in you!

I believe you are so close to your next level in life, whether it is spiritual, family or business, it's so close, it's at your fingertips!

Grab hold of what is meant for you and what you want, please don't let it slip away!

I know there is a plan & a purpose for you.

I often speak about "Your Journey" A journey is more than about waking up each day & going to work, school, etc.

A journey is about making & accomplishing small attainable goals that will help you get to the Big Goal!

A journey is a road map of the purpose meant for your life! You are so much more than an idle thought. There is so much to your life than you could ever imagine!

You are so much more than an idle thought. There is so much to your life than you could ever imagine!

Encouraging you to really seek your purpose for being upon this earth. Learn why you were given another chance to see a new day!

Despite what anyone has to say, it is never too late to start your journey.

What I have come to understand is that I'm just where HE HAS ME TO BE!

Life never just happens!

Goals don't just land in our hands!

And dreams just don't appear!

I believe that they are seeds planted

that should be well nurtured!

One thing is for sure,

One plants,

One waters

but it is

God that gives the increase!

As I was getting settled in last night, preparing for my day these words fell on my heart:

If He allows me to see a new day, it is a fact that things are already better! No matter what you are facing, today is a chance to turn things around for your good.

As I write this, I am rejoicing that yes I made it through the night! I made it through a storm! I made it through some struggles. I made it through some disappointments! Yes, I made it through. I made it through so that I can share with you that all things are possible.

New chances are given, new opportunities to rethink your plans. Never assume it's just another day. It is more to it than that!

It may look like the odds are against you, but if you put forth some effort to turn things around, I am a believer as well as one that has walked in some shoes, that things will turn around just for you! Just because you made a positive effort for an effect change!

FINANCIAL

REFERENCE SCRIPTURES ON FINANCES

Luke 6:38

Proverbs 22:7

1 Timothy 5:8

1 Timothy 6:10-11

II Corinthians 9:6-15

Luke 16:11

Luke 14:28

James 1:17

Proverbs 13:22

Haggai 2:8

Proverbs 3:9-10

Philippians 4:19

Proverbs 21:20

Hebrews 13:5

How do we begin to touch this subject? So many times we find ourselves struggling with our finances. With all of our obligations of just living we must do two of the following things, follow the directions given concerning what is due unto God as well as to obey the laws of the land, which are God's instructions as well. One may ask what do you mean and how does it concern my finances? Our tithing is for the upkeep of the House of God, and we must pay to live upon this earth. There is no simpler way to put it.

How can this be? How am I supposed to give unto God as well as obey the laws of the land? It is something that we must all grow unto, please don't pretend that this has always come easy for you, because it does not. Therefore we are posed with the question are we really giving all unto God that is due? It is more than just our time, attention, heart, mind, soul, praise & worship but we are to give of monetary values as well. Yes, we are to pay our tithes and offerings. It does not negate that we have an opinion of what we give but that we give from our hearts. When we give unto God from our hearts He will in turn supply all of our needs according to His riches and glory, not that man should repay us for this which is our reasonable service. This is a walk of faith! Faith that as I do according to the word of God and give unto Him that He will supply all that I need. We can't become stingy with what we have yet expected God to give unto us so freely, this just does not work. Have we tried it, just be honest, yes we have. If we are to fully understand any of this, than we are giving because we are showing gratitude for His many blessings!

We often struggle in our finances because we miss-use our provisions, and then we go to God to bail us out. Yes, it is true that He will give us the desires of our heart but we must learn how to handle what He allows us to have. Sometimes we find ourselves in a struggle when we move into another level because we never learned how to handle the previous level, this is true as well, if you can't handle the little then you are going to struggle when more comes. So there are all of these alarming questions, "why do I keep finding myself here in this financial struggle"? Why is it that I can't seem to grow beyond this point?

There are several answers to these questions.

1. Are we living beyond our means?

2. 2. Are we placing our wants before our needs? Are we looking for others to bail us out while we spend how we want to spend?

3. Do we have a spirit of paying things late?

4. Are we under the assumption that others owe us something, therefore we don't have to put forth an effort of working for what we want?

5. When you go to God for guidance and help, are our hands clean in giving unto Him what belongs to Him? I am learning to give thanks, ask for forgiveness before I ask of anything.

When we learn to acknowledge what we did to end up on this side of the struggle, then I believe that God will move on our behalf. But at what point do we want to come up out of this struggle? So then there comes a bigger question, what are you doing with the gifts God gave you to earn an income? Ouch! Let's take it a step further, as parents what are we teaching our children concerning financial struggles so that they do not repeat our patterns?

On the next few pages, we have provided some space for you to write down the financial areas you are having issues with. Each page has been labeled with a specific area as well as some blank pages for the things that are not listed.

Please really take the time and look over your pattern of living and how you would like to make some positive changes. Of course take these things to God in prayer, that He may lead and guide you. Feel free to do this exercise as an individual, a family or in a group discussion.

There is one page that has struck a cord, I need financial structure, this is something that the word of God teaches us about and it works, if we would apply the instructions.

One thing is for certain, financial security does not mean you are blessed, having the favor of God is being blessed!

I AM HAVING A ISSUE PAYING MY TITHE

I AM SPENDING ON MY WANTS BEFORE MY NEEDS

I HAVE NOTHING TO SHOW FOR MY INCOME

I WANT MORE BUT I CAN'T HANDLE WHAT I HAVE NOW

_____

_____

_____

_____

_____

_____

_____

_____

_____

_____

_____

_____

_____

_____

_____

_____

_____

_____

_____

_____

I NEED FINANCIAL STRUCTURE

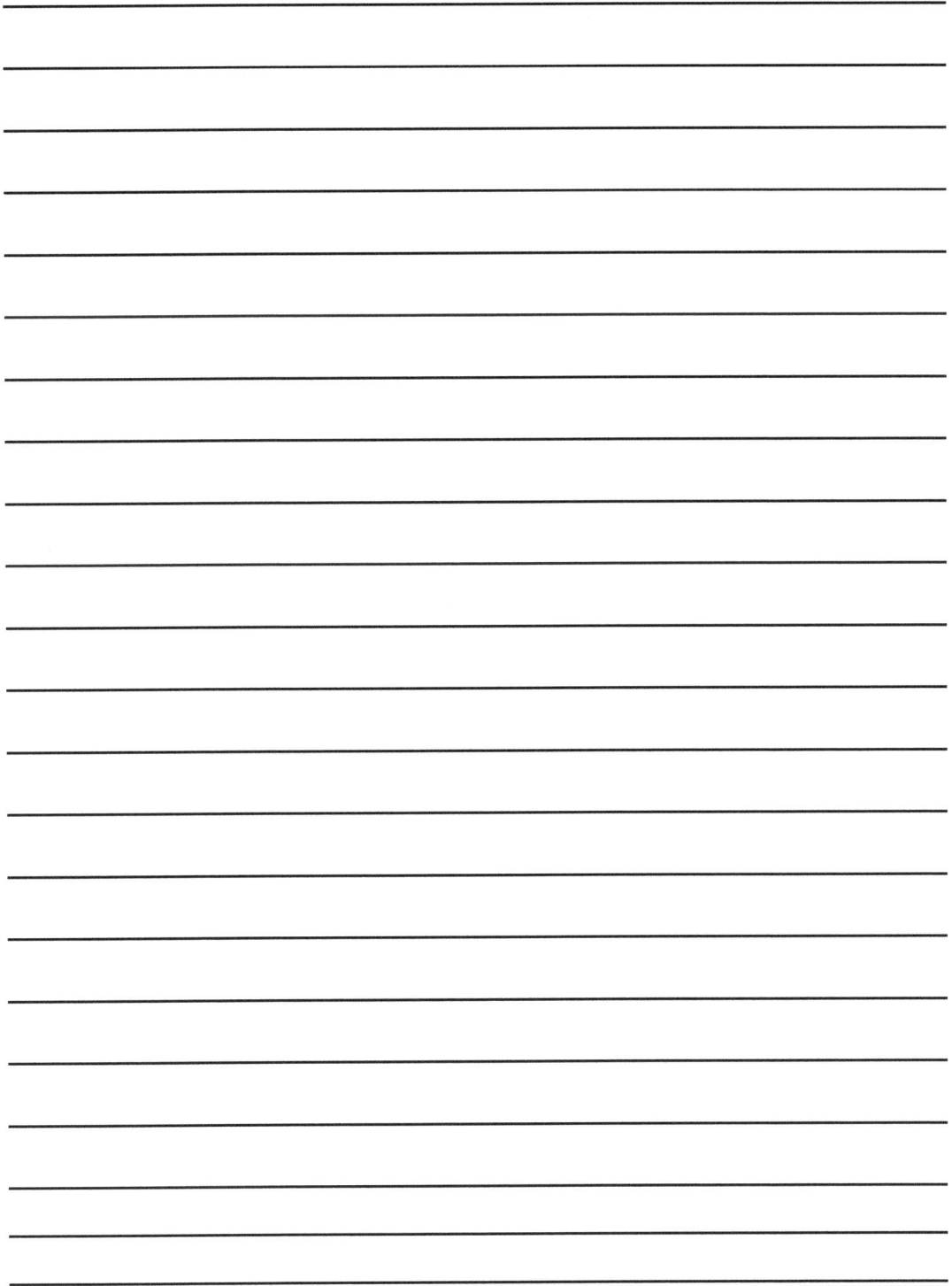

RELATIONSHIPS

REFERENCE SCRIPTURES ON RELATIONSHIPS

Hosea 12:6

Matthew 23:23

Luke 11:42

Psalm 89:14

Deuteronomy 32:4

Hebrews 13:4

Malachi 2:11

Matthew 5:27-28

Exodus 20:14

Ephesians 5:33

Ruth 1:16-18

Ruth 2:11-12

1 Samuel 2:19

1 Samuel 23:16

Galatians 6:10

Sometimes things come at us without warning. And when those things come, they hit hard.

The truth is that those things hit with an impact that can knock us off of our feet. We might even shed a tear or two.

But it's these things that helps us to grow. It's the things that causes us pain to recognize what is best for us.

When you are growing in maturity, you will begin to look at the errors you made in the things that went wrong.

There is a truth about coming into maturity, it will make you look at the things & people that hurt you differently.

It will make you accept your responsibility. Maturity will make you look at yourself! Maturity will make you realize that you gave others the tools to hurt you!

This journey of maturity will make you go to God for reassurance instead of man.

Don't get me wrong, I love people but no one can understand the things I can't put into words but the one that created me.

Family, in the mist of your hurt & misunderstandings, as you are looking for answers. Look within, all you need is there waiting…………………………………………………………

Once you accept what is there, the pain will not hurt as bad. You will get up a lot sooner as there is no time to sit and wallow in self-pity.

But of course take all caution to the wind that blows and the next time you will move with open eyes instead of a wounded heart!

Decisions!

Before you relax today, really think about your present state. Is this where you want to be?

Are you ever going to grow tired of looking for someone else to pull you out!

Sometimes we become comfortable looking to others.

But I am a firm believer we all carry a conscious decision of should I try and stand on my own two feet, taking responsibility for myself or am I going to rely on others because I know they will!

If I could shake trees that are holding captive the will & drive that I know is within you, my arms would never tire! It's time for a wakeup call family!

We keep crying for help from the comfort our sofas, refusing to open the doors of opportunity that continues to call out to you.

Please don't ignore the tap that turned into a loud knock that is now pounding begging you to give your life & purpose a try.

Things could be so much better for us, but only if we want it

Developing A Plan of Action

As you are pursuing your future, I encourage you to create a plan of action and stick to it.

Never become discouraged because the road ahead has a lot of bumps, twists & turns.

In order to reach those goals no matter the size, we all need a plan to bring them into a reality.

Create a business plan today for your life!

It's all about taking one step at a time, surrounding yourself with those that are supportive.

Make sure you are involved with those that have gone & achieved where you are going.

Here is an exercise & a few questions to consider:

Take a look at your current circumstances. Are you satisfied? Are you content? Now, ask yourself, where would you like to be in 6 months to a year.

Now consider what will it take to get there! I say go for it, you can do! I believe in the potential within you!

No matter what you are facing this morning or even yesterday, encouraging you to look forward.

I am learning that as I move forward in life that I must rely on the guidance of God.

Once I go to Him with an issue, I have to believe that His directions are for the best.

Sometimes we can override those instructions because we think we know best.

But allow me to tell you from some very personal experiences, it is better to follow His way.

For He can see beyond what we can even imagine!

And what I love about His guidance, is that it's not filled with a bunch of opinions or it will not become the topic at the next gathering!

Your life is not about what I think you should do with it but what He sees as what's the very best for you!

Timing! Timing is everything.

The effectiveness of your journey determines your patience of time!

Within my journey, I am learning to observe timing!

Yes, I have been early, I have been late. Let's not dare to admit that I have been eager as well as slow.

I am learning not to look at the end of things but during the beginning of the process, that my time is not his time!

I am learning to move with caution and care. For when I rush, things did not measure up.

There have been occasions that I wanted it NOW! But I was not counting the full cost of having it in the now.

Here is what I know, that all things will work out but we must be willing to wait the full course of time for all things to come to pass.

We can't rush the birth of the seed to bloom into a plentiful harvest. For if we rush the seed, the seed is synthetic and not real. You will not produce much, only more synthetics! Yet a seed of truth, held in the right timing, is a harvest that will be of benefit to others rather than just ourselves.

For if only I can enjoy the harvest, then I am full of greed and selfishness alone! But the seed is meant for others as well that we all become feed with unlimited nourishment!

Morning Inspirations

I must admit that I am in love with my journey! It brings me into reality.

Not the reality that fits me but the reality of me!

I am in pursuit of understanding me!

I am in that era of accepting the things I have done

& not so much as to what was done unto me.

I am more interested in making sure I don't cross certain lines,

you know "staying in my lane."

Here is something that hit me hard this weekend as I was working,

maturity does not mean that you are better than the next person.

Maturity is simply a reminder for us to think before we react.

Maturity tells me that before I can move forward

I must be willing to accept my role in all things.

Maturity tells me that if I want my journey to continue in the right path

that some roads I have no choice but to forsake.

Yes, I am at the crossroads of moving to another level.

I am far from perfect and I never want that desire.

For the perfect have no room for growth.

I need to forever learn! For the more I learn the more I see that I need to learn!

Stay encouraged, encouraging others along the way!

Author Angel Ferguson

Something to share, I used to get annoyed by the things that seem to keep repeating themselves in my life! My first thought was "Been there done that" Yet now I have come to realize that those things were being repeated because I was missing the lesson! I would not accept the lesson, because let's face it, I wanted it my way.......... When I can hear that inner voice that screams, "here it comes again" with any given situation, it's because I have allowed it to be so! The reality is that as soon as you accept that your journey is about you, the less circles you will have to go in! & You will begin to recognize the distractions that come to shake your focus. Simply put, don't run from maturity! It's there to guide you through to your designed destination.

There is an art to moving on... What may work for me may not work for you........................... But there is one thing that is true, when that hunger and desire for change won't go away we all eventually have to satisfy that need! Encouraging you to understand that need. Is this need for the better? Who will this change effect? Is this change apart of my purpose? To me change is the definition of correcting a mistake. In short no method is perfect. We all have to discover the right canvas, colors & paint brush in order to paint the scenes of our personal journeys.

Here we are in another area on our journey, exploring the reality of truth! Understanding that we often times ask for that which we are unwilling to GIVE! Let's be real, we all have that double standard of, "I am giving you the truth of what I need you to know!" I have the understanding that before anything or anyone I need to be honest & truthful with God then to myself. For if I am honest with God, he will reveal to me the truth of me! What I am learning is this; how can I expect trust & truth if I can not understand it & the power it holds! Here is another truth, we allow others to treat us based off of how we treat ourselves. For if I am not honest with myself how can I expect the next person to be honest with me? So today, do the unexpected and become truthful with yourself! Recognize where you truly are! Accept it! Then decide if you are truly satis-fied. But within your soul searching, understand this, NO ONE IS RE-SPONSIBLE FOR YOUR HAPPINESS & FULFILLMENT BUT YOU!

NOTES SECTION

NOTES SECTION

NOTES SECTION

NOTES SECTION

<u>NOTES SECTION</u>

The purpose behind this book is to help us become aware of our everyday lives. Sometimes we can't recognize things as a struggle because we have accepted them as normal, when in fact we can have a better live, in Christ. We pray that you have found the information and examples within this book helpful as you pursue a closer relationship with Christ. That you take the time to discover the things in your life that you seem to struggle with and that you go to God for the solutions for a true freedom in Him!

No one has all the answers, but we believe that what we do need is found in the word of God.

Stay encouraged, encouraging others along the way during your journey upon this earth!

Apostle Namon Wilson Jr.

&

Motivational Speaker Angel Ferguson

ABOUT THE AUTHORS

Apostle Namon Wilson Jr., is the founder of

Charity Lighthouse of Faith.

This great ministry has grown to reach souls internationally.

Apostle Wilson, is the husband of Pastor Valerie Wilson, a father, a business owner and a teacher of the true gospel of Jesus Christ.

Angel Ferguson is the founder of Hope & Truth Magazine, an author of several books & business owner.

Above all Angel is a mother first, grandmother, a writer than a motivational speaker.

www.ingramcontent.com/pod-product-compliance
Lightning Source LLC
Chambersburg PA
CBHW041425090426
42741CB00002B/33